The Scottish Collection

Classic
MALTS

CAROL P. SHAW

HarperCollins*Publishers*

HarperCollins Publishers
PO Box, Glasgow G4 0NB

First published 1997

Reprint 10 9 8 7 6 5 4 3 2 1 0

© HarperCollins Publishers, 1997

ISBN 0 00 472068 7

A catalogue record for this book is available from the British Library

Printed and bound in Italy by Rotolito Lombarda S.p.A., Pioltello

CONTENTS

The Classic Malts

Contents (contd)

Distilleries featured in this book

ORKNEY

Kirkwall Highland Park
Scapa

John o' Groats
Wick

Clynelish

Glenmorangie
Dalmore
Teaninich
Glen Ord   Nairn   Macduff
Inverness   Peterhead
Royal   SPEYSIDE
Brackla (See pp.6–7)
Tomatin   Glengarioch

SKYE   Aberdeen

Talisker

Dalwhinnie   Royal
Lochnagar
Blair Athol   Fettercairn
Fort William   Lochside
Ben Nevis   Edradour
HIGHLAND   Montrose

Tobermory   Aberfeldy

MULL

Oban   Dundee
Glenturret   Perth
TAY
Tullibardine
Deanston
Stirling
FORTH
Glengoyne
Bunnahabhain   Dumbarton
Isle of Jura   Littlemill Auchentoshan   Edinburgh
Caol Ila Bowmore
ISLAY   Glasgow
Bruichladdich   LOWLAND   Glenkinchie
Lagavulin
Laphroaig   Peebles
CAMPBELTOWN   CLYDE
Glen Scotia Campbeltown
Springbank   Ayr

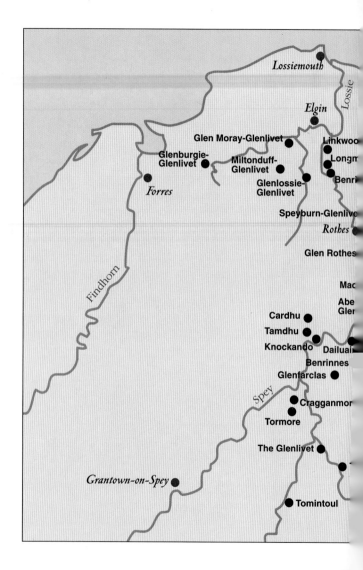

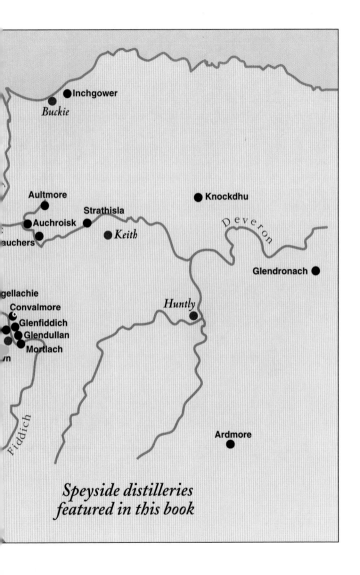

Inchgower
Buckie

Aultmore
Strathisla
Auchroisk
auchers
Keith

Knockdhu

D e v e r o n

Glendronach

gellachie
Convalmore
Glenfiddich
Glendullan
Mortlach
vn

Huntly

Fiddich

Ardmore

*Speyside distilleries
featured in this book*

TASTE RATING

The descriptions of the different whiskies which follow contain a taste rating. The figures shown are not intended to be a judgement on the quality or relative standard of the spirit, nor is it possible to place strength and flavour together satisfactorily. Rather, it can be used as an indicator of accessibility of the whisky for a relatively inexperienced palate. A whisky may be mild or strong and still either lack flavour or exude it, so this rating concerns the degree of flavour, while at the same time allowing for the strength interfering with a person's ability to appreciate the flavour. The basic categories are as follows:

1	Popular with particular palates; spirituous, with a very mild flavour
2	Good for beginners; appealing taste and flavour for most palates at certain times
2–3	Also good for beginners, but a little stronger than 2. One to return to again and again
3	A dram for everyone; not too powerful, with pleasant sensations
3–4	This should also appeal to most tastes, but is slightly stronger, so the palate requires a little more experience
4	Very pleasing; a stronger spirit, ideal for those with more experience
5	Robust; only for the well-developed palate

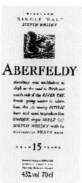

ABERFELDY

Aberfeldy Distillery, Aberfeldy, Perthshire

BOTTLING AGE...	15 years	TASTE RATING ...	3
STRENGTH.......	43%	MINIATURES	Yes

Tasting Notes

Basically a dry malt with a medium body and clean, fresh character, but with a distinctly peaty background.

Aberfeldy Distillery stands near the River Tay, at the town from which it takes its name. Building began in 1896 and the distillery opened two years later. It was built by Dewar but passed with that company into the ownership of the Distillers Company Ltd in 1925. Almost all of its production now goes into United Distillers' blends, most notably Dewar's White Label. The single malt is still relatively rare, only becoming available in official bottlings in the Distillery (Flora and Fauna) Malts series early in the 1990s.

ABERLOUR

Aberlour-Glenlivet Distillery, Aberlour, Banffshire

BOTTLING AGE . . . 10, 12 years TASTE RATING . . . 3

STRENGTH . . . . . . 40%, 43% MINIATURES . . . . . Yes

Tasting Notes
A smooth, rich, sherried Speyside malt which is an ideal after-dinner drink.

Established in the 1860s, Aberlour Distillery was rebuilt in the early 1880s after its destruction in a fire. It sits below Ben Rinnes from whose slopes it draws its water, said to be an important characteristic of its distinctive flavour. In the distillery grounds is the well of St Drostan (or Dunstan), the tenth-century missionary and patron saint of Aberlour who later became Archbishop of Canterbury. Since its acquisition by the Pernod Ricard company in 1974, Aberlour has been well marketed in France, where it is one of the most popular of Scotch whiskies. The company also owns the Irish Distillers Group.

AN CNOC

Knockdhu Distillery, Knock, Banffshire

BOTTLING AGE... 12 years   TASTE RATING ... 2–3

STRENGTH....... 40%   MINIATURES ..... Yes

Tasting Notes

An Cnoc's dryish aroma is complemented by a mellow sweetness in the flavour. This Highland malt was previously known as Knockdhu.

Knockdhu Distillery was established in 1893 on a favoured site: with water available from Knock Hill, barley from the nearby farmlands, and a good supply of local peat. Although both its buildings and machinery have since been modified, the production process remains essentially the same, with the two originally designed pot stills remaining. Previously owned by the Distillers Company Ltd and licensed to Haig, Knockdhu was sold in 1988 to Inver House Distillers, who reopened it after a lengthy silent period. Its single malt is one of the few which does not take its distillery's name.

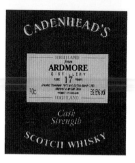

ARDMORE

Ardmore Distillery, Kennethmont, Aberdeenshire

BOTTLING AGE... Varies		TASTE RATING ... 4	
STRENGTH...... Varies		MINIATURES..... Yes	

Tasting Notes

A full-bodied Speyside malt which is both robust and sweet. An ideal after-dinner dram, although it is not easy to come by; available as a single malt only through independent bottlers.

The distillery at Ardmore was built in 1898 by the Teacher family of whisky merchants and blenders. Since that time almost all its production has gone into Teacher's blends, most famously Highland Cream. Today it is operated by Allied Distillers, so its product also features prominently in Allied's other blends. Although the distillery has been modernized it still retains some of the original equipment, such as coal-fired stills, which were used in the production of whisky at the end of the nineteenth century.

AUCHENTOSHAN

Auchentoshan Distillery, Dalmuir, Dunbartonshire

BOTTLING AGE.. 10, 21 years   TASTE RATING .. 2–3

STRENGTH......40%, 43%   MINIATURES .... Yes

Tasting Notes

A light, sweetish whisky whose smooth qualities are perhaps partially owed to the process of triple, rather than the more common double distillation.

Although Auchentoshan Distillery lies south of the Highland Line (the line initiated by the Customs and Excise to differentiate area boundaries between styles of whisky), it uses water from north of the line, so theoretically could be said to have a foot in both camps. It is, however, officially recognized as a Lowland distillery and whisky. Founded in the early nineteenth century, part of its interesting history includes surviving bombing in the Clydebank Blitz during the Second World War, when a stream of blazing whisky was said to have flowed from the building. It is presently owned by Morrison Bowmore, also owners of Bowmore and Glen Garioch distilleries.

SPEYSIDE
SINGLE MALT *SCOTCH WHISKY*

AULTMORE

distillery located between *KEITH* and *BUCKIE* began production in
1897. The name, derived from the *Gaelic*, means *"big burn"*.
Ideal supplies of *water* and *peat* from the *Foggie Moss* made this area
a haunt of *illicit distillers* in the past. *Water* from the *Burn* of
AUCHINDERRAN is now used to produce this *smooth, well balanced*
single *MALT* *Ye SCOTCH WHISKY* with a *mellow* finish.

A G E D 12 Y E A R S

43% vol Distilled & Bottled in SCOTLAND. AULTMORE DISTILLERY Keith, Banffshire, Scotland. 70 cl

AULTMORE

Aultmore Distillery, Aultmore, Keith, Banffshire

BOTTLING AGE . . . 12 years   TASTE RATING . . . 3

STRENGTH . . . . 43%   MINIATURES . . . . . Yes

Tasting Notes

A faintly peaty aroma leads into this smooth, fruity, well-
balanced whisky which has become – deservedly – better
known in recent years.

Aultmore Distillery was established in 1895 at the tail-
end of the whisky boom by the owner of the older
Benrinnes Distillery. The area, with its abundant peat and
water supplies, was infamous in the past for illicit distilling.
Peat used in the production process is taken from a nearby moss, and the water is taken from local springs. The
distillery passed to Dewars in 1923, and was improved and
upgraded in the 1970s. It is now owned by United
Distillers who have been officially bottling its single malt in
their Distillery (Flora and Fauna) Malts series since the
early 1990s.

BALMENACH

Balmenach Distillery, Cromdale, Moray

BOTTLING AGE . . . 12 years	TASTE RATING . . . 4
STRENGTH 43%	MINIATURES . . . . . Yes

Tasting Notes

A complicated, full-bodied malt, best suited as an after-dinner dram.

The Balmenach Distillery, in the Haughs of Cromdale, is set in an area which was notorious for illicit distilling for many years before the Licensing Act of 1823. Built in 1824 by James McGregor (great-grandfather of Sir Robert Bruce Lockhart, author of the classic 1951 book, *Scotch*), Balmenach was one of the first distilleries in the Highlands to be licensed under the 1823 act. The distillery was acquired by United Distillers and most of its production went into the company's blends but has since been closed. The single malt is still relatively rare, only becoming available in official bottlings in the Distillery (Flora and Fauna) Malts series early in the 1990s.

THE BALVENIE

Balvenie Distillery, Dufftown, Keith, Banffshire

BOTTLING AGE . . 10, 12, 15 years   TASTE RATING . . 3–4

STRENGTH . . . . . .Varies   MINIATURES . . . . Yes

Tasting Notes

Founder's Reserve (10-years-old) has a rich colour, bouquet and flavour with a smooth, clean, dry finish. Doublewood (12-years-old) is full-bodied, yet smooth and mellow, and Single Barrel, a harder-to-obtain 15-year-old, is a single-cask bottling.

Built in 1892 near the ruins of fourteenth-century Balvenie Castle by the Grants of Glenfiddich (and next to the Glenfiddich distillery), Balvenie Distillery has now been owned by an independent family company for five generations. Balvenie Distillery still grows its own barley, malts in its own traditional floor maltings, employs coopers to tend the barrels and coppersmiths to tend the stills. The Balvenie is most unusual in producing a range of three malt whiskies of different age and character.

BEN NEVIS

Ben Nevis Distillery, Fort William, Inverness-shire

BOTTLING AGE. 19, 25, 26 years TASTE RATING . . . 3

STRENGTH . . . . . Varies MINIATURES . . . . . No

Tasting Notes

Ranging from pale amber to a deep, golden colour, Ben Nevis is characterized by its fresh, slightly peaty flavour and smooth finish.

Ben Nevis Distillery, standing at the foot of Scotland's highest mountain, is one of the oldest distilleries in Scotland. It was founded at Fort William by the famous local character, 'Long' John Macdonald in 1825. (The brand name of Long John and the distillery company became separated.) After more than 100 years and three generations in the family, the distillery was sold in 1941. The subsequent addition of a patent still made the distillery one of the few that could produce both malt and grain under one roof, and it received a new lease of life in the late 1980s following its acquisition by the Nikka Whisky Distilling Co. of Japan.

BENRIACH

Benriach Distillery, Longmorn, Elgin, Moray

BOTTLING AGE . . . 10 years	TASTE RATING . . . 4
STRENGTH 43%	MINIATURES . . . . . Yes

Tasting Notes

A medium-bodied, fruity whisky with sweetish overtones and a gently malty finish. A new bottling has been available from the distillery since 1994.

Originally built in 1898, Benriach was closed in 1900, after recession hit the previously booming whisky industry. It was refitted and reopened in 1965, although not completely modernized, still retaining its hand-turned malting floor. The company is owned by Seagram, and most of its produce goes into their blends. Although the distillery now produces its own, official bottling, this is still not an easy whisky to come across.

BENRINNES

Benrinnes Distillery, Aberlour, Banffshire

BOTTLING AGE... 15 years		TASTE RATING ... 4	
STRENGTH...... 43%		MINIATURES ..... Yes	

Tasting Notes

This is a complex Speyside malt which has hints of wood and grass to its flavour, and a fruity aftertaste.

Built almost 700 feet up the slopes of Ben Rinnes, from which it takes its name, this distillery is believed to have been founded in 1835 although evidence exists of distilling on this site in 1826. It was largely rebuilt and modernized in the 1950s. Most of its production is distilled three times rather than the more usual twice, and almost all is used in United Distillers' blends. The single malt is still relatively rare, only becoming available in official bottlings in the Distillery (Flora and Fauna) Malts series early in the 1990s.

BLADNOCH

Bladnoch Distillery, Bladnoch, Wigtown, Wigtownshire

BOTTLING AGE . . . 10 years	TASTE RATING . . . 3
STRENGTH 43%	MINIATURES . . . . . Yes

Tasting Notes

Bladnoch is a light-to-medium-bodied malt with a light, fragrant, lemony aroma and a gentle, unassertive flavour with fruity tones.

Bladnoch was Scotland's most southerly distillery, in Wigtownshire, and was also one of its oldest. It was built in 1817 and stood on the banks of the River Bladnoch, in the village of the same name. It had many owners throughout the course of the twentieth century, the latest being United Distillers. The distillery is now closed. Bladnoch's single malt is still relatively rare, only becoming available in official bottlings in UD's Distillery (Flora and Fauna) Malts series early in the 1990.

BLAIR ATHOL

Blair Athol Distillery, Pitlochry, Perthshire

BOTTLING AGE . . . 12 years	TASTE RATING . . . 2–3
STRENGTH 43%	MINIATURES . . . . . Yes

Tasting Notes

A light, fresh malt with dry notes, a hint of smokiness and strong fruit overtones, leading into a very smooth finish.

This is a picturesquely sited distillery on a wooded hillside on the outskirts of the pretty Perthshire tourist centre of Pitlochry. Blair Athol is unusual in that it is twelve miles distant from the village after which it is named. Established in 1825, the distillery was bought by Bell in 1933 and sympathetically upgraded, although it did not produce again for another 16 years. It is now owned by United Distillers. Its water comes from the Allt Dour (Burn of the Otter) which flows past the distillery en route to the River Tummel.

BOWMORE

Bowmore Distillery, Bowmore, Islay, Argyll

BOTTLING AGE . .	12, 17, 21, 22, 25, 30 years	TASTE RATING . .	3
STRENGTH	40%, 43%	MINIATURES	Yes

Tasting Notes

With its pleasant aroma and peaty–fruity flavour, Bowmore is a good Islay malt for newcomers to these distinctive whiskies to try.

Established in the 1770s, Bowmore is reputed to be the oldest legal distillery on Islay. It stands in the island's main town and overlooks Loch Indaal, and its water is taken from the peaty River Laggan. The distillery has passed through several hands in the twentieth century, but it has been a consistently thriving concern since its acquisition in 1963 by Stanley P. Morrison of Glasgow. The company is now Morrison Bowmore, and this is their flagship distillery.

The
BRUICHLADDICH
ISLAY
Single Malt
SCOTCH WHISKY

DISTILLED, MATURED AND BOTTLED BY
BRUICHLADDICH DISTILLERY COMPANY LIMITED
BRUICHLADDICH, ISLE OF ISLAY, SCOTLAND

AGED 10 YEARS

70cl   40%vol

BRUICHLADDICH

Bruichladdich Distillery, Bruichladdich, Islay, Argyll

BOTTLING AGE . . 10, 15, 21 years   TASTE RATING . . 3

STRENGTH . . . . . 40%, 43%   MINIATURES . . . Yes

Tasting Notes

A subtle malt, and less medicinal in its flavour than other Islay whiskies, Bruichladdich is a lightish, dry, fresh-tasting whisky.

Built in 1881, Bruichladdich is Scotland's most westerly distillery. Its water comes from an inland reservoir and, unlike the other distilleries, is not drawn from springs which have flowed over peaty land; this has been suggested as a reason why its peaty flavour is less intense than other Islay malts. Bruichladdich was owned by Invergordon Distillers from 1972 until 1993, but since the company's acquisition that year by Whyte & Mackay, it has been mothballed along with two of the group's other distilleries, Tamnavulin and Tullibardine.

BUNNAHABHAIN

Bunnahabhain Distillery, Port Askaig, Islay, Argyll

BOTTLING AGE... 12 years

STRENGTH...... 40%

TASTE RATING... 3

MINIATURES..... Yes

Tasting Notes

Less characteristically peaty than some other Islay malts, Bunnahabhain is a mellow whisky with an aromatic flavour, and a smooth, long finish.

Bunnahabhain, on the north shore of Islay, is one of the more isolated of the island's distilleries. Founded in 1881, it has changed very little in the intervening century despite expansion in the 1960s. All its production formerly went into blends. Bunnahabhain was owned by the Islay Distillery Company who bought Glen Rothes Distillery in 1887, together forming the Highland Distilleries Company. They still own Bunnahabhain today.

BUSHMILLS 5 YEARS OLD MALT

Old Bushmills Distillery, Bushmills, Co. Antrim

BOTTLING AGE . . . 5 years   TASTE RATING . . . 2

STRENGTH . . . . 40%   MINIATURES . . . . . Yes

Tasting Notes

A smooth, nicely balanced Irish malt which is both light and sweet. This is ideal as an aperitif.

Although it was only one of many distilleries in an area which was also famous for its abundant poteen production, Bushmills has emerged as the region's only survivor. Its increasingly strong trading position saw it benefit from industry rationalization in the second half of the twentieth century, as in its gradual swallowing-up of the operations of Coleraine Distillery, and it has emerged from its amalgamations with the promise of a secure future.

BUSHMILLS 10 YEARS OLD MALT

Old Bushmills Distillery, Bushmills, Co. Antrim

BOTTLING AGE... 10 years   TASTE RATING ... 2–3

STRENGTH....... 40%   MINIATURES ..... Yes

Tasting Notes

Light and delicately sweet, Bushmills Malt has a rich, malty flavour and a pleasingly dry finish.

Old Bushmills Distillery is the world's oldest legal distillery and at the backbone of its survival and successes has been the quality of the spirit it has produced, with a portfolio of distinguished whiskies across the production spectrum. In 1897 the distillery marked Queen Victoria's diamond jubilee by its first production of pure malt, specially produced whiskey which retailed at fifty shillings a case! For many years in the past century Bushmills proudly proclaimed its status as Ireland's only producer of single malt.

CAOL ILA

Caol Ila Distillery, Port Askaig, Islay, Argyll

BOTTLING AGE . . . 15 years	TASTE RATING . . . 4
STRENGTH 43%	MINIATURES . . . . . Yes

Tasting Notes

Nicely balanced, Caol Ila is pleasantly peaty with a sweet edge and a well-rounded body.

Caol Ila was established in 1846 and overlooks the Sound of Islay (which is also the English translation of its name). It previously used its own wharf for the despatching of its product. The distillery has been rebuilt twice, at almost 100-year intervals, in 1879 and 1972. The most recent modernization almost doubled the distillery's output. Caol Ila is now owned by United Distillers. The single malt is still relatively rare, only becoming available in official bottlings in UD's Distillery (Flora and Fauna) Malts series early in the 1990s.

CARDHU

Cardhu Distillery, Knockando, Moray

BOTTLING AGE... 12 years	TASTE RATING ... 2–3
STRENGTH...... 40%	MINIATURES ..... Yes

Tasting Notes

A smooth, light malt of silky character and delicate, sweet flavour which make it accessible to all from the novice to the connoisseur.

Whisky distilling had been carried on illegally in the Knockando area for a long time before Cardow Distillery, as it was then, was founded and licensed in 1824. The distillery was bought by John Walker of Kilmarnock during the boom years of the 1890s, producing a vatted and a single malt under the Cardhu name. It was modernized in 1965 and its single malt was relaunched, with the distillery name being changed in 1981 to match that of its product. It is now owned by United Distillers. Cardhu enjoys a splendid situation overlooking the Spey valley and has recently been refurbished.

CLYNELISH

Clynelish Distillery, Brora, Sutherland

BOTTLING AGE... 14 years   TASTE RATING... 3

STRENGTH...... 43%   MINIATURES..... Yes

Tasting Notes

Clynelish is a medium-bodied, full-flavoured whisky. It is slightly dry to the taste, with a hint of peat.

The original distillery at Brora was built by the 1st Duke of Sutherland, the prime mover in the most infamous of the Highland Clearances. Its purpose was to make full use of the cheap grain grown on the new coastal farms of his newly-cleared tenants. A new distillery was built on adjacent land in 1967–68, taking the name Clynelish, while the original distillery, now renamed Brora, was closed by the Distillers Company Ltd, its parent company, in 1983. It is now owned by United Distillers.

PURE POT STILL
Connemara

PEATED SINGLE MALT
40% vol. **IRISH WHISKEY** 75 cl e

Distilled, Matured & Bottled in Ireland, Cooley Distillery Plc, Riverstown, Dundalk, Co. Louth

• PRODUCT OF IRELAND •

CONNEMARA

Cooley Distillery, Dundalk, Co. Louth

STRENGTH . . . . 40%   TASTE RATING . . . 2–3

MINIATURES . . . . . No

Tasting Notes

A drier single malt than Tyrconnell, its sister from the Cooley stable, this is a smooth, medium-bodied whiskey. Its soft and unassertive peaty flavour betrays its unique position as Ireland's only peated single malt.

Launched in 1996, Connemara is one of the newest brands from the forward-looking young Cooley Distillery, which began production in 1989. Formerly Ceimici Teo Distillery, it was bought in 1987 by entrepreneur John Teeling who had been keen for several years to enter the whiskey market. The takeover by Pernod Ricard of the Irish Distillers Group in the same year meant that by the time the Cooley Distillery whiskies came of age in 1992 after their required three-year maturation period, they offered the sole alternative to the Pernod/IDG monopoly. The Cooley whiskies are shipped by road to mature in oak-cask-filled warehouses at the old Locke's Distillery buildings in Kilbeggan, Co. Westmeath.

The Best of Speyside

CRAGGANMORE

MALT

SINGLE HIGHLAND MALT

AGED 12 YEARS

Scotch Whisky

AN ELEGANT, SOPHISTICATED SPEYSIDE with the most complex aroma of any malt. Astonishingly fragrant with sweetish notes and a smoky maltiness on the finish.

40%vol

70cl e

SPECIALLY BOTTLED IN SCOTLAND FOR THE CRAGGANMORE DISTILLERY, BALLINDALLOCH, BANFFSHIRE

CRAGGANMORE

Cragganmore Distillery, Ballindalloch, Banffshire

BOTTLING AGE... 12 years

STRENGTH...... 40%

TASTE RATING ... 3–4

MINIATURES ..... Yes

Tasting Notes

A malt of distinctive and complex character, Cragganmore has a delicate smoky aroma and long, clean finish.

Cragganmore was built in 1869 and was the first distillery to be constructed alongside an existing railway and so utilise the then new mode of transport for distribution. The distillery took its name from nearby Craggan More Hill. It was built by John Smith (a man of great bulk, also known locally as 'Cragganmore') and is now licensed to D. & J. McCallum. Most of its production goes into blends, especially Old Parr, and until a few years ago, the single malt was only infrequently available. The distillery is owned by United Distillers.

CRAIGELLACHIE

Craigellachie Distillery, Craigellachie, Banffshire

BOTTLING AGE . . . 14 years   TASTE RATING . . . 3

STRENGTH . . . . 43%   MINIATURES . . . . . Yes

Tasting Notes

A smoky-smelling and -tasting malt of medium body, Craig-ellachie works well as an after-dinner dram.

This distillery is pleasantly situated on high ground above the River Spey outside Dufftown. It was built in 1891 by the Craigellachie Distillery Co., a founder of which was Peter Mackie, the creator of the White Horse brand. Mackie and Co. (later White Horse Distillers) subsequently bought the distillery in 1915. It is now owned by United Distillers and most of its production is devoted to blending. The single malt is still relatively rare, only becoming available in official bottlings in the Distillery (Flora and Fauna) Malts series early in the 1990s.

SPEYSIDE
SINGLE MALT *SCOTCH WHISKY*

DAILUAINE

is the GAELIC for "the green vale". The *distillery*, established
in 1852, lies in a hollow by the *CARRON BURN* in *BANFFSHIRE*. This
single Malt Scotch Whisky has a *full bodied fruity* nose and a *smoky* finish.
For more than a *hundred years* all *distillery supplies* were despatched by
rail. The *steam locomotive* "DAILUAINE NO.1" was in use
from 1939~1967 and is *preserved* on the *STRATHSPEY RAILWAY*.

AGED **16** YEARS

43% vol   Distilled & Bottled in SCOTLAND. DAILUAINE DISTILLERY, Carron, Aberlour, Banffshire, Scotland.   70cl

DAILUAINE

Dailulaine Distillery, Carron, Banffshire

BOTTLING AGE . . . 16 years   TASTE RATING . . . 4

STRENGTH . . . . 43%   MINIATURES . . . . . Yes

Tasting Notes

A full-bodied malt, with a heathery and sweetish flavour.

Dailuaine Distillery stands near the Spey below Ben
Rinnes and was established in 1851 by William
Mackenzie; it was subsequently taken over by his son,
Thomas, and greatly expanded during the 1880s. The
distillery was one several owned by the Dailuaine-Talisker
Distillery Co., an amalgamated company formed by
Mackenzie. Its current owners are United Distillers and
most of its produce goes into their blends, such as Johnnie
Walker. Consequently its single malt is still relatively rare,
and has only become available in official bottlings in the
Distillery (Flora and Fauna) Malts series early in the 1990s.

THE DALMORE

Dalmore Distillery, Alness, Ross-shire

BOTTLING AGE . . . 12 years

STRENGTH 40%

TASTE RATING . . . 4

MINIATURES . . . . . Yes

Tasting Notes

A smooth, full-bodied whisky with a hint of sherry and peat in its malted flavours. A good digestif.

Built in 1839, Dalmore Distillery was bought in 1867 by the Mackenzie family, although ownership has now passed to Whyte & Mackay. Much of its produce today goes into Whyte & Mackay blends. The distillery is attractively set in a picturesque location with a wooded, hilly backdrop and outlook over the Cromarty Firth to the fertile Black Isle. This location led to a break in the production of whisky during the First World War when the American navy took over the distillery and its access to the deepwater Cromarty Firth, for the manufacture of mines.

DALWHINNIE

Dalwhinnie Distillery, Dalwhinnie, Inverness-shire

BOTTLING AGE . . . 15 years	TASTE RATING . . . 2-3
STRENGTH 43%	MINIATURES . . . . . Yes

Tasting Notes

Ideal as a pre- or post-dinner dram, Dalwhinnie is light and aromatic with a soft, heather-honey finish.

Built in 1898 at the end of the boom years for the whisky industry, Dalwhinnie Distillery was called Strathspey when it first opened, even though it was not, strictly speaking, on Speyside. It stands on the Drumochter Pass at a height of more than 1000 feet, close to pure water sources, and was for many years Scotland's highest distillery. It is presently owned by United Distillers. Most of its output went to blending until 1988 when the Dalwhinnie single malt was developed.

DEANSTON

Deanston Distillery, Doune, Perthshire

BOTTLING AGE . . . 12, 17 years TASTE RATING . . . 3

STRENGTH . . . . . . 40% MINIATURES . . . . . Yes

Tasting Notes

A light, fresh, smooth Highland malt with a sweetish, fruity flavour.

Originally a cotton mill dating from 1785, Deanston was converted to a whisky distillery in 1966. Water for distilling and electricity comes from the River Teith that rises north of Loch Lomond and flows through the Trossachs. The mill's original weaving sheds, with their humidity control and their temperature, are perfect for maturing the whisky and are considered to add a natural smoothness to its character. Deanston was bought by Burn Stewart of Glasgow in 1991.

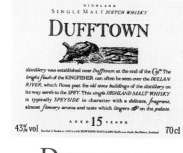

HIGHLAND
SINGLE MALT *SCOTCH WHISKY*

DUFFTOWN

distillery was established near *Dufftown* at the end of the C9th The *bright flash* of the KINGFISHER can often be seen over the *DULLAN RIVER*, which flows past the old stone buildings of the *distillery* on its way *north* to the *SPEY*. This *single HIGHLAND MALT WHISKY* is typically *SPEYSIDE* in character with a *delicate, fragrant,* almost *flowery* aroma and taste which *lingers* on the *palate*.

AGED **15** YEARS

43% vol   70cl
Distilled & Bottled in HIGHLAND DUFFTOWN DISTILLERY Dufftown, Keith, Banffshire, Scotland

DUFFTOWN

Dufftown Distillery, Dufftown, Keith, Banffshire

BOTTLING AGE... 15 years   TASTE RATING ... 2-3

STRENGTH...... 43%   MINIATURES..... Yes

Tasting Notes

A pleasant Speyside malt with a delicate, fragrant aroma which is almost flowery, and a smooth, sweet taste. Doubles as a before- or after-dinner dram.

Prettily situated at the water's edge in the Dullan Glen, this is one of seven distilleries in and around Dufftown, a major whisky production centre. There were disputes in the early years over water rights, some of which led to the nocturnal diversion and re-diversion of local supplies. The distillery finally gained the right to draw its supplies from Jock's Well, a reliable source of fine, sweet water some distance away. The single malt is still relatively rare, becoming more widely available in official bottlings in United Distillers' Distillery (Flora and Fauna) Malts series early in the 1990s.

THE EDRADOUR

Edradour Distillery, Pitlochry, Perthshire

BOTTLING AGE... 10 years   TASTE RATING ... 3

STRENGTH....... 40%   MINIATURES..... Yes

Tasting Notes

A smooth Highland malt with pleasant notes of fruit and malt in its taste, complemented by a slight dryness.

Edradour is Scotland's smallest distillery, as well as being one of its most picturesque. Built in 1837, it stands on the steep banks of a burn in the Perthshire countryside, and sympathetic modernization in 1982 left its appearance unchanged. The distillery had been bought by William Whiteley in 1933 and, despite a takeover in 1982 by Pernod Ricard subsidiary, the House of Campbell, Whiteley still hold the licence. Most of the malt goes into Campbell blends, and it is only since 1986 that it has been available as a single malt under the distillery label.

SINGLE HIGHLAND MALT

GLENBURGIE

TRADE MARK OF PROPRIETORS: J G STODART LTD.

SCOTCH WHISKY

40% VOL.   AGED 8 YEARS   70cl

PRODUCT OF SCOTLAND

*Specially selected, produced and
bottled by and under the responsibility of*
GORDON & MACPHAIL
Elgin, Scotland. Regd. Bottler.

GLENBURGIE

The Glenburgie-Glenlivet Distillery, Forres, Moray

BOTTLING AGE . . . Varies

STRENGTH . . . . . . Varies

TASTE RATING . . . 3

MINIATURES . . . . . Yes

Tasting Notes

A light-bodied, delicate single malt whose sweet, slightly floral taste makes it ideal as an aperitif.

A distillery was said to have been established here in 1810, but production ceased and was not revived until the second half of the nineteenth century. It was bought by James & George Stodart Ltd of Dumbarton who themselves were taken over by Hiram Walker in the 1930s. The distillery was extended in 1958 and is now owned by Allied Distillers, with most of its produce going into their blends. Because of this, Glenburgie can be difficult to find.

GLEN DEVERON

Macduff Distillery, Banff, Banffshire

BOTTLING AGE . . . 12 years		TASTE RATING . . . 3–4	
STRENGTH 40%		MINIATURES . . . . . Yes	

Tasting Notes

A very pleasant Highland malt with a smooth, mellow taste and fresh bouquet.

A modern distillery, built in 1962, Macduff is one of the few distilleries to give its single malt a different name from its own (although independent bottlers do market the whisky, including miniatures, under the name of 'Macduff'). The malt takes its names from the nearby River Deveron from which is drawn the water used for cooling in the production process. Macduff Distillery is now owned by William Lawson Distillers, a subsidiary of Bacardi Ltd, Bermuda.

GLENDRONACH

The Glendronach Distillery, Forgue, Huntly, Aberdeenshire

BOTTLING AGE...	12 years	TASTE RATING ...	3
STRENGTH......	40%, 43%	MINIATURES	Yes

Tasting Notes

Glendronach is a beautifully rounded malt whose slight peaty tones are balanced by a lingering smoky sweetness.

This distillery, set picturesquely on the Dronach Burn in the Aberdeenshire countryside, is one of the most attractive in the Highlands. Built in 1826, it was one of the first to be licensed, and its whisky enjoyed a wide reputation in the nineteenth century. Its original hand-turned malting floor and coal-fired stills have been retained. Since 1960 it has been operated by William Teacher & Sons, with produce going into the Teacher's blends. It has been owned since 1988 by Allied Distillers who have temporarily suspended production.

SPEYSIDE
SINGLE MALT
SCOTCH WHISKY

GLENDULLAN

distillery, located in a beautiful wooded
valley was ... built in 1897 and is one of seven
established in Dufftown is the 6th
The River Fiddich flows past the distillery,
originally providing power to drive
machinery, it is now used for cooling.
GLENDULLAN is a firm, mellow single MALT
SCOTCH WHISKY with a fruity
bouquet and a smooth, lingering finish.

AGED 12 YEARS

43% vol   70 cl

GLENDULLAN

Glendullan Distillery, Dufftown, Keith, Banffshire

BOTTLING AGE... 12 years   TASTE RATING ... 3

STRENGTH...... 43%   MINIATURES..... Yes

Tasting Notes

A good single malt with a robust character yet a mellow, fruity flavour.

This is one of the seven Dufftown distilleries, built just before the turn of the century and picturesquely set on the banks of the Fiddich. Built for William Williams of Aberdeen, it passed to the control of Macdonald Greenlees & Williams after the First World War and, with its parent company, into the ownership of the Distillers Company Ltd in 1926. Rebuilt in 1962, it is now owned by United Distillers and its single malt is still relatively rare, although it has been officially bottled in the Distillery (Flora and Fauna) Malts series. Glendullan is also an important component of the Old Parr and President blends.

GLENFARCLAS

Glenfarclas Distillery, Marypark, Ballindalloch, Banffshire

BOTTLING AGE . . 10, 12, 15, 21, 25, 30 years

TASTE RATING . 3–4, 5(60%)

STRENGTH 40%, 43%, 46%, 60%

MINIATURES . . . Yes

Tasting Notes

A classic malt with a rich, sherry bouquet, a well-rounded, fruity body and a delicious, mellow finish.

Glenfarclas is one of the few independently owned distilleries left in the Highlands. Founded in 1836, it was bought in 1865 by J. & G. Grant (who were no direct relations of the family of Grants at Glenfiddich) and is still in family hands. Glenfarclas bottles a wide range of malts of varying ages and strengths. The distillery is set in an isolated spot by Ben Rinnes yet it attracts in excess of 60,000 visitors a year to its well-maintained visitor facilities.

GLENFIDDICH

Glenfiddich Distillery, Dufftown, Banffshire

BOTTLING AGE . . No age given   TASTE RATING . . . 2

STRENGTH . . . . . 40%   MINIATURES . . . . . Yes

Tasting Notes

Glenfiddich has a light, peaty aroma with a smooth, counterbalancing sweetness.

Glenfiddich Distillery was started by William Grant, a former apprentice shoemaker who worked at Mortlach, another Dufftown distillery, until he gained enough knowledge and money to set up on his own in 1887. The new distillery was successful as soon as it went into production, and has remained so ever since, thanks not only to the quality and accessibility of its product but also to far-sighted marketing which has made its single malt possibly the best-known in the world. The distillery is part of the largest family-owned independent whisky company.

GLEN GARIOCH

Glen Garioch Distillery, Oldmeldrum, Aberdeenshire

BOTTLING AGE . . 9, 15, 21 years TASTE RATING . . . 3

STRENGTH . . . . . 40%, 43%   MINIATURES . . . . . Yes

Tasting Notes

This medium-bodied whisky, with its light texture and smoky flavour, is an ideal after-dinner dram.

Set in the small Aberdeenshire market town of Oldmeldrum, Glen Garioch was reputedly founded in the 1790s. It has had several owners throughout its history, and was sold by the Distillers Company Ltd in 1970 to Morrison, two years after its closure because of a shortage of water. Having sunk a new well, Morrison were able to tap sufficient sources of spring water to enable normal production to continue. The distillery has now been moth-balled and its long-term future seems uncertain.

THE UNPEATED MALT
FROM THE SOUTHERN HIGHLANDS

PRODUCT OF SCOTLAND

GLENGOYNE

SINGLE HIGHLAND MALT
SCOTCH WHISKY

DISTILLED MATURED & BOTTLED BY
LANG BROTHERS LIMITED
DUMGOYNE SCOTLAND

THE OLD GLEN GUIN

In the quiet, secluded glen
beneath the Hill of Dumgoyne,
Glengoyne Distillery
captures the essence of the
soft air and the cool Glengoyne
burn water that flows into Loch
Lomond to craft this unpeated
malt Scotch whisky.

GLENGOYNE

Glengoyne Distillery, Dumgoyne, Stirlingshire

BOTTLING AGE . . 10, 12, 17 years   TASTE RATING . . 2–3

STRENGTH . . . . . 40%, 43%   MINIATURES . . . Yes

Tasting Notes

A light, pleasant, sweetish whisky with a fragrant aroma and no abrasive edges. Ideal as an aperitif.

Glengoyne stands just north of the Highland Line (the line initiated by the Customs and Excise to differentiate area boundaries between styles of whisky) and so qualifies as a Highland distillery. It was built in 1833 at the foot of the Campsie Fells, near the fifty-foot waterfall from which it takes its supplies. It was bought by Lang Brothers in 1876 and was sympathetically restored and extended in the 1960s. Glengoyne is the least peated Scottish malt.

GLEN GRANT

Glen Grant Distillery, Rothes, Moray

BOTTLING AGE . . 5, 10 years   TASTE RATING . . 2

STRENGTH . . . . . . 40%, 43%   MINIATURES . . . Yes

Tasting Notes

The 5-years-old is light and dry, making it ideal as an aperitif, while the older version has a sweeter, fruitier, and more rounded character.

Opened by James and John Grant in 1840, Glen Grant enjoyed continuous expansion throughout the last century, and this has continued to the present day, with its number of stills doubling to eight in the 1970s. The company was amalgamated with the Smiths of Glenlivet in the 1950s to form The Glenlivet and Glen Grant Distillers, which in turn merged with the Edinburgh blending firm of Hill Thomson in 1970 to form The Glenlivet Distillers. Glen Grant is now part of Seagram. The distillery's five-years-old single malt is the best-selling malt whisky in Italy.

GLENKINCHIE

Glenkinchie Distillery, Pencaitland, Tranet, East Lothian

BOTTLING AGE... 10 years

STRENGTH...... 43%

TASTE RATING ... 3

MINIATURES ..... Yes

Tasting Notes

Ideal as an aperitif, Glenkinchie is the driest and smokiest of Lowland whiskies. It is a pleasantly peaty, smooth whisky.

Glenkinchie takes its name from the burn which flows by it and the glen in which it stands. It was established in the late 1830s by the Rate brothers. The licence is held by John Haig & Co., the brand owned by United Distillers, and most of Glenkinchie's product goes into their blends, particularly the bestselling Haig. The single malt was officially bottled by United Distillers in their Classic Malts series.

THE GLENLIVET

The Glenlivet Distillery, Ballindalloch, Banffshire

BOTTLING AGE . . 12, 18, 21 years   TASTE RATING . . 3–4

STRENGTH . . . . . . 40%, 43%   MINIATURES . . . . Yes

Tasting Notes

The Glenlivet is a subtly balanced malt. Its light, delicate bouquet has traces of fruit, and floral notes, while the complex flavours are delicately balanced between a medium sweetness and smooth dryness.

This was one of the first distilleries licensed under the reforming 1823 Licensing Act – a fact which so incensed his still-illegal neighbours that its founder, George Smith, was obliged to carry pistols for his own protection. The whisky so grew in popularity that other distillers adopted the name, and an ensuing legal case and settlement (which endures to this day) allowed the Smiths to use the direct article in their whisky's name while others were to use it as a hyphenated suffix.

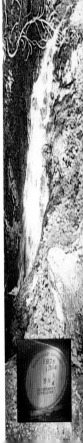

SPEYSIDE
SINGLE MALT *SCOTCH WHISKY*

The three *spirit stills* at the

GLENLOSSIE

distillery have *purifiers* installed between the *lyne arm* and the
condenser. This has a bearing on the *character* of the *single*
MALT *SCOTCH WHISKY* produced which has a *fresh, grassy*
aroma and a *smooth*, lingering flavour. Built in 1876 by *John Duff*,
the *distillery* lies four miles *south* of ELGIN in *Morayshire*.

AGED **10** YEARS

43% vol   70 cl

GLENLOSSIE

Glenlossie-Glenlivet Distillery, Elgin, Moray

BOTTLING AGE . . . 10 years   TASTE RATING . . . 2

STRENGTH . . . . . . 43%   MINIATURES . . . . . Yes

Tasting Notes

Glenlossie has a fresh, grassy aroma with a touch of
fruitiness and a smooth, lingering flavour.

Glenlossie was built not far from the River Lossie in
1876 by a former distillery manager-turned-hotel
owner from Lhanbryde, near Elgin. It was expanded and
improved between 1896 and 1917. In 1962, its stills were
increased from four to six, while in 1992 a new mash tun
was fitted. The licensee is presently Haig and the distillery
is owned by United Distillers. The single malt is still
relatively rare, but became available in official bottlings in
UD's Distillery (Flora and Fauna) Malts series early in the
1990s.

GLENMORANGIE

Glenmorangie Distillery, Tain, Ross-shire

BOTTLING AGE . . . 10, 18 years   TASTE RATING . . . 3–4

STRENGTH . . . . 40%, 43%   MINIATURES . . . . . Yes

Tasting Notes

A smooth and medium-bodied whisky, with a delicate, slightly sweet aroma.

Distilling was begun here in 1843 by the Mathieson family as a sideline to farming. In 1918, The Glenmorangie Distillery Company passed into the control of its present owners, Macdonald and Muir Ltd. Water is supplied by unusually hard, mineral-rich springs in nearby Tarlogie Forest, and the lightly peated new spirit is distilled in Glenmorangie's characteristically tall, swan-necked stills, before being transferred into charred American oak barrels or the maturation process.

GLENMORANGIE
PORT WOOD FINISH

Glenmorangie Distillery, Tain, Ross-shire

BOTTLING AGE . . Min. 12 years   TASTE RATING . . . 3

STRENGTH . . . . . 43%   MINIATURES . . . . . Yes

Tasting Notes

This whisky has a sweet aroma with minty notes and a dry, very smooth taste. The port flavours of the final maturing come through on the lingering and quite satisfying finish.

This malt is one of a series of newcomers to Glenmorangie's single malts range. In its final 'finishing' period of maturation, the whisky is transferred not into the usual charred American oak bourbon barrels, but into casks which have previously contained port. This second wood imparts its own new qualities which enhance without overpowering, the delicate and subtle core flavours. Glenmorangie also produce two other single malts which have been finished in Madeira and sherry casks.

GLEN MORAY

Glen Moray-Glenlivet Distillery, Elgin, Moray

BOTTLING AGE . . . 12, 15 years   TASTE RATING . . . 2–3
STRENGTH . . . . 40%, 43%   MINIATURES . . . . . Yes

Tasting Notes

Golden in colour, with a soft, fresh bouquet leading into a smooth, medium-sweet and rounded taste, Glen Moray is a classic Speyside malt.

Established during the whisky boom years of the 1890s, the Glen Moray-Glenlivet Distillery was closed in 1910 but was expanded in 1958 from two to four stills. Since the 1920s it has been owned by Macdonald & Muir Ltd and, in addition to its availability as a single malt, its produce also features in many well-known blends in their portfolio. Glen Moray is the sister distillery to the better-known Glenmorangie.

GLEN ORD

Glen Ord Distillery, Muir of Ord, Ross-shire

BOTTLING AGE...	12 years	TASTE RATING...	2–3
STRENGTH......	40%	MINIATURES.....	Yes

Tasting Notes

A smooth, well-rounded and slightly dry malt with a fragrant, lightly peated bouquet and mellow finish.

This distillery stands in an area which was infamous for illicit distillation even as late as a century ago. It stands on a tributary of the River Conan, the Oran Burn, whose clear waters have been used by legal and illegal whisky producers alike. Ord Distillery, as it then was, was founded in 1838 on land leased from the Mackenzies of Ord to provide a ready market for barley produced on Mackenzie farms. It was acquired by Dewar in 1923, and is now owned by United Distillers, having been extensively rebuilt and enlarged in the mid 1960s.

THE GLENROTHES

Glen Rothes Distillery, Rothes, Moray

BOTTLING AGE... Varies	TASTE RATING... 3–4
STRENGTH...... 43%	MINIATURES..... Yes

Tasting Notes

A popular, full-bodied single malt with a delicate, lightly peated aroma and a pleasingly smooth aftertaste.

The Glen Rothes Distillery was built in 1878 for William Grant & Sons with the backing of a group of local businessmen, including the provost of Rothes. It was bought in 1887 by the Islay Distillery Company, owners of Bunnahabhain, and then became part of the Highland Distilleries company. They still own the distillery today. Glen Rothes has been expanded twice in the last thirty years. The Glen Rothes single malt is produced and distributed by Berry Brothers & Rudd, the owners of Cutty Sark whisky, in which Glen Rothes also features.

GLEN SCOTIA

Glen Scotia Distillery, Campbeltown, Argyll

BOTTLING AGE... 12 years   TASTE RATING ... 3

STRENGTH...... 40%   MINIATURES ..... Yes

Tasting Notes

Glen Scotia is a rich, peaty, oily malt with a pungent aroma and a smooth, well-rounded finish.

Scotia, as it was previously known, was one of thirty-two Campbeltown distilleries operating last century, partly explaining why the town has its own regional classification, even though only two distilleries remain. Glen Scotia Distillery was built in 1835 and has had many owners, the ghost of one of whom is said to haunt the place. It is currently owned by Loch Lomond Distillery Co. Ltd, the owners of Loch Lomond Distillery and the producers of Inchmurrin single malt. Both Glen Scotia and its sister distillery, Littlemill at Bowling, have now been mothballed.

GLENTAUCHERS

Glentauchers Distillery, Mulben, Banffshire

BOTTLING AGE ... Varies   TASTE RATING ... 2

STRENGTH ...... 40%   MINIATURES ..... Yes

Tasting Notes

A rich, fruity and delicately peated malt, the sweetness of Glentauchers' aroma and taste are balanced by the light dryness of its finish.

Glentauchers was built in 1898 by James Buchanan, the entrepreneur responsible for the success of Black & White whisky, and its product went into their blends. Buchanan's distillery was largely rebuilt and modernized in 1965 but was silent for several years in the 1980s until Allied Distillers acquired it from United Distillers in 1988 and immediately reopened it.

THE GLENTURRET

Glenturret Distillery, The Hosh, Crieff, Perthshire

BOTTLING AGE . 12, 15, 21, 25 years   TASTE RATING . 3–4

STRENGTH . . . . . 40%   MINIATURES . . Yes

Tasting Notes

Glenturret is a full-bodied Highland malt with a rich, lightly peated, nutty flavour and nicely rounded finish.

Glenturret stands in a lovely position on the banks of the River Turret, in an area where smuggling and illicit distillation were rife in the past. It is probable that the distillery's own eighteenth-century origins lie there; some of its buildings date from that time. Glenturret was closed and partially dismantled in the 1920s and was silent until 1959, when it was largely rebuilt, anticipating the huge upswing in demand for blended whiskies in the 1960s. Today its visitor facilities are among the best of any Scots whisky distillery.

HIGHLAND PARK

Highland Park Distillery, Kirkwall, Orkney

BOTTLING AGE . . . 12 years	TASTE RATING . . . 3–4
STRENGTH 40%	MINIATURES . . . . . Yes

Tasting Notes

Highland Park is a medium-bodied single malt of character, with a heathery–smoky aroma and a dryish, peaty flavour with balancing sweet tones.

Highland Park's origins are linked with an illegal bothy which previously occupied the site. Its owner was one of whisky's most colourful characters, Magnus Eunson. A United Presbyterian church elder by day and smuggler by night, his piety did not prevent his using the church pulpit as a handy hiding place for his illicit distillations. The distillery was founded in 1798 and passed to the Grant family in 1895. Highland Distilleries purchased it in 1937. The different nature of Orcadian peat is said to be a factor in the quite distinctive qualities of the islands' whiskies. Highland Park is the more widely available of the islands' two malts.

The *Oyster Catcher* is a common sight around the

INCHGOWER

distillery which stands close to the sea on the mouth of the RIVER SPEY near BUCKIE. Inchgower, established in 1871, produces one of the most distinctive single malt whiskies in SPEYSIDE. It is a malt for the discerning drinker ~ a complex aroma precedes a fruity, spicy taste ~ with a hint of salt.

A G E D **14** Y E A R S

43% vol   70cl

INCHGOWER

Inchgower Distillery, Buckie, Banffshire

BOTTLING AGE . . . 14 years   TASTE RATING . . . 2–3

STRENGTH . . . . 43%   MINIATURES . . . . . Yes

Tasting Notes

A robust, distinctly heavy-bodied malt with a combination of nutty, fruity and spicy aromas, and a hint of sweetness in its tones.

Inchgower Distillery was moved from Tochineal by its founder, Alexander Wilson, to its present site at Rathaven near Buckie, to take advantage of the ready supply of water from the Letter Burn and the Springs of Aultmoor. When the original firm went out of business, the distillery passed to Buckie Town Council who sold it to Arthur Bell & Sons for £1000 in 1938. Most of the whisky goes into Bell's blends and the distillery is now owned by United Distillers.

INCHMURRIN

Loch Lomond Distillery, Alexandria, Dunbartonshire

BOTTLING AGE... 10 years   TASTE RATING ... 2

STRENGTH....... 40%   MINIATURES ..... Yes

Tasting Notes

A clean, light, pre-dinner malt with fresh, floral notes amidst its dry, quite spirity flavours.

A relatively recent addition to the ranks of Scotland's distilleries, Loch Lomond Distillery was founded in 1966 on the site of an old printing and bleaching plant. Like Glengoyne, it just qualifies as being a Highland malt and is situated just to the south of the famous loch. A grain distillery also shares the site. Its present owners, Loch Lomond Distillery Co., recently took control of two more malt distilleries, Littlemill at Bowling and Glen Scotia in Campbeltown, both of which are currently mothballed.

ISLE OF JURA

Isle of Jura Distillery, Craighouse, Jura, Argyll

BOTTLING AGE . . . 10 years   TASTE RATING . . . 3

STRENGTH . . . . . . 40%, 43%   MINIATURES . . . . . Yes

Tasting Notes

Isle of Jura has a clean, light and slightly dry palate with delicate smoky notes and a smooth finish.

The distillery is one of the main employers on this island of around 200 inhabitants. It was first built overlooking the Sound of Jura in 1810, next to a cave where illicit distillation may have carried on for up to three centuries. The distillery's machinery and buildings were owned by different individuals, and a dispute between the two led to its closure for over fifty years from 1913. It was effectively redesigned and rebuilt before its reopening in the 1960s. The present owners are Whyte & Mackay who acquired it, and six other malt distilleries, after their purchase of Invergordon Distillers in 1993.

KNOCKANDO

Knockando Distillery, Knockando, Aberlour, Banffshire

BOTTLING AGE . . . Min. 12 years. TASTE RATING . . 3–4

STRENGTH . . . . 43%   MINIATURES . . . Yes

Tasting Notes

Knockando is a lightly peated malt, with pleasantly smooth, sweet hints amongst its rich, fresh flavours.

Built during the 1890s whisky boom, Knockando is today owned by International Distillers and Vintners. The distillery's name is said to mean 'small black hill', and Knockando itself is set on a hill overlooking the Spey. Knockando single malt is bottled only when it is considered to have reached its peak rather than at a predetermined age – generally, this is between twelve and fifteen years. The label lists the year of distillation – the 'season' – and the year of bottling. Such season dating recalls the time when Scottish distilleries only distilled during the winter season after the barley harvest.

LAGAVULIN

Lagavulin Distillery, Port Ellen, Islay, Argyll

BOTTLING AGE . . . 16 years

STRENGTH 43%

TASTE RATING . . . 5

MINIATURES . . . . . Yes

Tasting Notes

A distinctively Islay malt, powerful and demanding, with a dominant aroma and a dry, peaty–smoky flavour complemented by a trace of sweetness.

Distilling was carried on in this area from the 1740s, when moonshiners made and smuggled illicit whisky to the mainland. Lagavulin's own history is entangled with these times, although the distillery dates officially from 1816. Peter Mackie, the main driving force behind the success of White Horse, started out on his distilling career at Lagavulin, and its produce was later to feature strongly in his blend. Lagavulin went into partnership with Mackie's company, subsequently the White Horse Company, and the whisky is still used in White Horse blends today. The distillery is owned by United Distillers

LAPHROAIG

SINGLE ISLAY MALT
SCOTCH WHISKY

10
Years Old

The most richly flavoured of
all Scotch whiskies

ESTABLISHED
1815

DISTILLED AND BOTTLED IN SCOTLAND BY
D. JOHNSTON & CO., (LAPHROAIG) LAPHROAIG DISTILLERY, ISLE OF ISLAY

40%vol   IMPORTENDOR WENCESLAO PAZ MARTÍNEZ
DOMICILIO C MADOD S/N B.S. NEW (03.1.125 ML   70cl

LAPHROAIG

Laphroaig Distillery, Port Ellen, Islay, Argyllshire

BOTTLING AGE . . . 10, 15 years   TASTE RATING . . . 5
STRENGTH . . . . . . 40%, 43%   MINIATURES . . . . . Yes

Tasting Notes

A robust, full-bodied, classic Islay malt with a trace of seaweed in its strongly peaty flavours.

Laphroaig Distillery is set on a bay on Islay's southern shore, and dates back to 1815. It is a traditional distillery and one of the few still to have a hand-turned malting floor, ensuring the traditional taste, generally held to be the most distinctive of all single malts. Enlarged several times during the 20th century, it is presently owned by Allied Distillers, for whom it is a top-five seller in the UK malts list and one of the top ten around the world. Laphroaig is also one of the components in their Long John, Ballantine's and Teacher's blends, as well as in the quality Black Bottle blend.

LEDAIG

SINGLE MALT
FROM
THE ISLE OF MULL

1974
Vintage

This rare old single malt whisky
was distilled at the Ledaig Distillery
on the Isle of Mull by
Ledaig Distillers (Tobermory) Ltd.

PRODUCE OF SCOTLAND

70cl   Sole agent for Switzerland   43%Vol
Jacques Vins et Spiritueux
Jacques Szmulovski Geneve.

LEDAIG

Tobermory Distillery, Tobermory, Mull, Argyll

BOTTLING AGE . . . 20, 21 years   TASTE RATING . . . 5

STRENGTH . . . . 43%   MINIATURES . . . . . No

Tasting Notes

A full-bodied single malt from the Tobermory Distillery, Ledaig has strongly peaty flavours.

Set in a wooded site by the sea, Tobermory Distillery has enjoyed mixed fortunes since it was first established in 1823. It has been closed several times during its existence, most recently in the 1980s when it was moth-balled. Having reopened in 1990, Tobermory is now back in production and it remains one of the few family-owned independent whisky distilleries. The distillery was previously known as Ledaig, changing its name in the 1970s. A single malt is also available under the distillery's new name of Tobermory.

LINKWOOD

Linwood Distillery, Elgin, Moray

BOTTLING AGE... 12 years   TASTE RATING ... 4–5

STRENGTH....... 43%   MINIATURES..... Yes

Tasting Notes

Linkwood is a full-bodied, smoky malt, with a fruity sweetness underlying its malty tones.

This is one of the most traditional of distilleries despite
extensive rebuilding work carried out three times since
its establishment in the 1820s: it is said that equipment was
never replaced until absolutely necessary, and even a
spider's web was not removed in case the change of
environment would affect the whisky! Built by a former
provost of Elgin, Linkwood has an attractive wooded
setting by Linkwood Burn outside the town. The distillery
is owned by United Distillers.

PRODUCT OF SCOTLAND

LITTLEMILL

Established 1772

SINGLE LOWLAND MALT
SCOTCH WHISKY

DISTILLED AND BOTTLED IN SCOTLAND BY
LITTLEMILL DISTILLERY CO. LTD.
BOWLING, DUNBARTONSHIRE, SCOTLAND

70cl ℮   40%vol

LITTLEMILL

Littlemill Distillery, Bowling, Dunbartonshire

BOTTLING AGE... 8 years   TASTE RATING ... 2–3

STRENGTH...... 40%   MINIATURES ..... Yes

Tasting Notes

A light Lowland malt with a smooth, sweet flavour. Its rich, clean finish makes it ideal as an aperitif.

Littlemill began life as a brewery centuries before distilling was started, with its ale apparently crossing the Clyde to supply the monks of Paisley Abbey. It was established as a distillery in the late eighteenth century and is one of the oldest in Scotland. Its water comes from the Kilpatrick Hills, to the north of the Highland Line (the line initiated by the Customs and Excise to differentiate the area boundaries between different styles of whisky), although Littlemill is a Lowland distillery and whisky. Owned until 1994 by Gibson International, it is now, with its sister distillery of Glen Scotia, under the control of the Loch Lomond Distillery Co., the producers of Inchmurrin single malt. Both Littlemill and Glen Scotia are presently mothballed.

LOCHSIDE

Lochside Distillery, Montrose, Angus

BOTTLING AGE...	10 years	TASTE RATING ...	2
STRENGTH.......	40%	MINIATURES	No

Tasting Notes

A light-to-medium-bodied single malt with a sweet, fruity aroma and drier, smooth flavour.

Established as recently as 1957, Lochside has been one of the shorter-lived Scotch whisky distilleries. It was built on the site of an eighteenth-century brewery and originally comprised two distilleries, one grain and one malt, as well as a blending plant. The distillery closed its grain-distilling and blending facilities in the late 1970s and continued in malt production only until 1992, when it was shut down completely by its Spanish owners. It is difficult to find under the distillery label, but supplies will continue to be available from independent merchants.

LONGMORN

Longmorn Distillery, Elgin, Moray

BOTTLING AGE . . 12, 15 years   TASTE RATING . 3–4

STRENGTH . . . . . . 40%, 43%, 45%   MINIATURES . . . Yes

Tasting Notes

Another classic Speyside malt of great character, Longmorn is a full-bodied whisky with a clean, fragrant aroma and a gently smoky, sweet taste.

The distillery was built by John Duff in 1894 on the site of an ancient chapel. Nearby is an old water wheel dating from the seventeenth century, although the distillery draws its water from a local spring. Longmorn, along with its sister distillery of Benriach, merged with The Glenlivet and Glen Grant Distilleries and Hill Thomson to form The Glenlivet Distillers. The distillery at that time was known as Longmorn-Glenlivet, but has now dropped its hyphenated suffix. Expanded in 1972 and 1974, the company was purchased by Seagram in 1976.

LONGROW

Springbank Distillery, Campbeltown, Argyll

BOTTLING AGE... 21 years   TASTE RATING ... 5

STRENGTH...... 46%   MINIATURES ..... Yes

Tasting Notes

A pungent malt produced using only peat-dried barley, which lends it a distinctive, peaty taste with an almost medicinal aroma and a complementary trace of sweetness.

Springbank Distillery produces Longrow as its second malt. It is called after another Campbeltown distillery of that name, which was closed in the late 1800s. The Longrow malt is so strongly peated that it has often been likened to an Islay malt. Springbank is unusual among Scots distilleries for several reasons: it is the only distillery-label malt which follows traditional techniques of not chill-filtering; it is the only distillery to carry out all production techniques on site; and it has been owned by the same family for close on two centuries.

THE MACALLAN

Macallan Distillery, Craigellachie, Banffshire

BOTTLING AGE . 7, 10, 12, 18, 25 years TASTE RATING . . . 3–4

STRENGTH . . . . 40%, 43%, 57% MINIATURES . . . Yes

Tasting Notes

Its rich, sherried aroma with a hint of peaches, its smooth, elegant flavour and its delightfully mellow aftertaste make the Macallan one of the most popular of malts

The Macallan's distinctive richness of taste and colour derives in part from its ageing in sweet sherry casks, a traditional practice which this distillery is the only one to maintain through all its range. The distillery itself originated on a farm set above a ford over the River Spey which was used by drovers travelling south. Distilling was probably under way on this site in the 1700s with the first licensed distilling taking place around 1824. It was bought and extended in 1892 by Richard Kemp, whose descendants owned the company until it was acquired by Highland Distilleries in 1996.

MILTONDUFF

Miltonduff-Glenlivet Distillery, Elgin, Moray

BOTTLING AGE...	12 years	TASTE RATING...	2–3
STRENGTH.......	40%, 43%	MINIATURES.....	No

Tasting Notes

A nice Speyside malt, medium-bodied and smooth, with a sweet and fragrant floral note.

Miltonduff-Glenlivet Distillery stands just to the south of Elgin near Pluscarden Abbey; the distillery's old mashhouse was said to have been built on the site of the abbey's brewery. The distillery itself was founded in 1824, and draws its water from the nearby Black Burn which flows down peaty Black Hill. Miltonduff was one of the original Hiram Walker distilleries acquired in 1937 and today is operated by Allied Distillers who use it in their blends, notably Ballantine's, and market the single particularly through duty-free outlets.

SPEYSIDE
SINGLE MALT
SCOTCH WHISKY

MORTLACH

was the first of seven
distilleries in Dufftown In the
0?° farm animals kept in
acpiring pyres were fed on
barley left over from processing.
Today water from springs in
the CONVAL HILLS is used to
produce this delightful
smooth, fruity single
MALT SCOTCH WHISKY.

AGED **16** YEARS

Distilled & Bottled in SCOTLAND
MORTLACH DISTILLERY
Dufftown, Keith, Banffshire, Scotland

43% vol 70cl

MORTLACH

Mortlach Distillery, Dufftown, Keith, Banffshire

BOTTLING AGE . . . 16 years   TASTE RATING . . . 4

STRENGTH . . . . . . 43%   MINIATURES . . . . . Yes

Tasting Notes

A Speyside malt of mellow, fruity flavour with a definite
peatiness and a dryness in the finish.

Another of Dufftown's distilleries, this time standing in
a little valley outside the town, by the River Dullan.
The distillery draws its water not from the river but from
springs in the local Conval Hills. Founded in 1823, it was,
in fact, the first of the distilleries to be built in the capital
of Speyside whisky-making, and it enjoyed a monopoly in
the town until 1887. The distillery has been modernized
twice this century and is now owned by United Distillers,
who did not officially bottle its malt until it featured in the
Distillery (Flora and Fauna) Malts series in the 1990s.

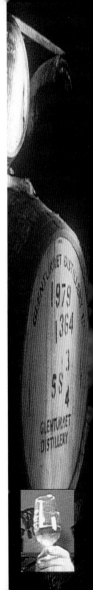

OBAN

Oban Distillery, Oban, Argyll

BOTTLING AGE...	14 years	TASTE RATING...	2–3
STRENGTH......	43%	MINIATURES.....	Yes

Tasting Notes

An intriguing, complex malt with a sweet and slightly peaty character which is balanced by a soft, dry finish.

First built as a brewery in 1794, Oban Distillery was part of the grand plan of the Stevensons, a family of energetic entrepreneurs and the founders of modern Oban at that time. The distillery, a grey building standing on the harbour front, draws its water from the Ardconnel area of peaty hills a mile from the town. It is licensed to John Hopkins, now owned by United Distillers, who currently feature the single in their Classic Malts series.

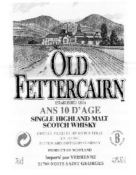

OLD FETTERCAIRN

Fettercairn Distillery, Fettercairn, Laurencekirk Kincardineshire

BOTTLING AGE... 10 years   TASTE RATING... 3–4

STRENGTH....... 40%, 43%   MINIATURES..... Yes

Tasting Notes

A smooth single malt with a full, malty taste and a satisfyingly dry counterbalance.

First established at its present location in 1824 by Sir Alexander Ramsay, Fettercairn is one of the country's oldest distilleries. Despite its age, it proved receptive to modern production methods when it became the first distillery in the country to use oil for heating its stills. It was once owned by John Gladstone, the father of the great Victorian prime minister W. E. Gladstone. Fettercairn is situated on the fringes of the Grampian Mountains, from which it takes its spring-water supplies. The distillery, which was extended in 1966, is presently owned by Whyte & Mackay.

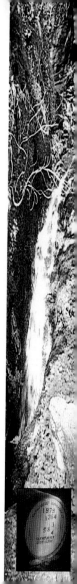

PITTYVAICH

Pittyvaich-Glenlivet Distillery, Dufftown, Keith, Banffshire

BOTTLING AGE... 12 years   TASTE RATING ... 4

STRENGTH...... 43%   MINIATURES..... Yes

Tasting Notes

Pittyvaich is a robust Speyside malt with a perfumed fruitiness underpinning a hint of spice and a strong aftertaste.

It was the success of neighbouring Dufftown-Glenlivet Distillery and the quality of its water supply, which encouraged Bell to build the brand-new Pittyvaich-Glenlivet Distillery almost next door, in 1974. Almost all of its product now goes into United Distillers' blends, and the single malt was difficult to find until it was officially bottled by UD as part of their Distillery (Flora and Fauna) Malts series. The distillery has now been closed.

LOWLAND
SINGLE MALT
SCOTCH WHISKY

Established on its present
site at CAMELON in 1840

ROSEBANK

distillers stands on the
banks of the FORTH
and CLYDE CANAL.
This was once
a busy thoroughfare with
boats and steamers
continually passing by;
it is still the source
of water for cooling.

This single MALT
SCOTCH WHISKY is
triple distilled which
accounts for its light
distinctive nose and well
balanced flavour.

AGED 12 YEARS

Distilled, Matured & Bottled at the
ROSEBANK DISTILLERY
Falkirk, Stirlingshire, Scotland

43% vol 70cl

ROSEBANK

Rosebank Distillery, Camelon, Falkirk, Stirlingshire

BOTTLING AGE... 12 years   TASTE RATING... 2

STRENGTH....... 43%   MINIATURES..... Yes

Tasting Notes

Rosebank is a smooth, mild whisky of light and medium-dry character, which makes it ideal as a pre-dinner dram.

Although a distillery was operating on this site in 1817, the most recent distillery generally dated from 1840, when much rebuilding took place. It stands on the banks of the Forth and Clyde Canal, on the outskirts of Falkirk. Triple distillation processes were used at Rosebank, which had one wash still and two spirit stills. The distillery is now closed. Its single malt was difficult to obtain, although it has been officially bottled in the Distillery (Flora and Fauna) Malts series.

HIGHLAND
SINGLE MALT SCOTCH WHISKY

ROYAL BRACKLA

distillery, established in 1812, *lies* on the *southern* shore of the MORAY FIRTH at *Cawdor* near Nairn. Woods around the *distillery* are home to the SISKIN; although a *shy bird*, it can often be seen *feeding* on conifer seeds.

In 1835 a *Royal Warrant* was granted to the *distillery* by King William IV, who enjoyed the *fresh, grassy, fruity* aroma of this *single malt* whisky.

43% vol   AGED **10** YEARS   70cl

Distilled & Bottled in SCOTLAND. ROYAL BRACKLA DISTILLERY, Cawdor, Nairn, Scotland.

ROYAL BRACKLA

Royal Brackla Distillery, Cawdor, Nairnshire

BOTTLING AGE . . . 10 years   TASTE RATING . . . 4

STRENGTH . . . . 43%   MINIATURES . . . . . Yes

Tasting Notes

A light, fresh, grassy malt with a hint of fruitiness and peat.

While William IV was known to have enjoyed Brackla's whisky, the distillery has been allowed officially to call itself 'Royal' since 1838, when his neice, the new queen Victoria granted it a Royal Warrant. Founded in 1812, the distillery has been rebuilt and extended several times in the past two centuries, although it is currently mothballed. It is licensed to Bissets, now owned by United Distillers, and almost all of its produce goes into their blends.

ROYAL LOCHNAGAR

Royal Lochnagar Distillery, Crathie, Aberdeenshire

BOTTLING AGE... 12 years	STRENGTH...... 40%
TASTE RATING ... 3–4	MINIATURES..... Yes

Tasting Notes

A big-bodied, rich and highly fruity malt with a delightfully sherried flavour. Royal Lochnagar Selected Reserve, with a more robust taste, is also available.

Lochnagar Distillery was built in 1826 by James Robertson, an infamous local illicit distiller, on the slopes of the mountain from which it took its name. Distilling was not peaceful work at that time: Lochnagar was destroyed by fire, reputedly the work of rival illicit distillers, in 1841 before being taken over and rebuilt by John Begg four years later Its 'Royal' prefix came after a visit and tasting in 1848 by Queen Victoria (who was said to be partial to whisky) and Prince Albert, who were staying at nearby Balmoral. The distillery was bought by Dewar, is now owned by United Distillers and is licensed to John Begg Ltd.

PURE MALT SCOTCH WHISKY
from
SCAPA
(ORKNEY)
Distillery
Proprietors: Taylor & Ferguson Ltd.

Bottled by Wm. Cadenhead,
75 cl   18 Golden Square, Aberdeen   46% vol
Scotland

SCAPA

Scapa Distillery, Kirkwall, Orkney

BOTTLING AGE. . . Varies   TASTE RATING . . . 3

STRENGTH. . . . . . Varies%   MINIATURES . . . . . Yes

Tasting Notes

A medium-bodied malt with a dryish, heathery flavour which is complemented by a satisfyingly malty sweetness.

Scapa is one of two distilleries in Kirkwall (Highland Park being the other), yet despite their proximity, their whiskies taste quite different. Scapa was built in 1885 by Macfarlane and Townsend – the latter already a well-known distiller on Speyside – and was bought by Hiram Walker in 1954. It is now owned by Allied Distillers who send most of its produce for blending, but also market the single largely through duty-free outlets. The distillery overlooks the giant natural bay of Scapa Flow, a major Royal Navy anchorage in both world wars and the site of the scuttling of the German fleet in 1918. The distillery was once saved from destruction by fire by ships in the bay.

THE SINGLETON OF AUCHROISK

Auchroisk Distillery, Mulben, Banffshire

BOTTLING AGE . . Min. 10 years   TASTE RATING . . . 2–3

STRENGTH . . . . . 40%   MINIATURES . . . . . Yes

Tasting Notes

This whisky is medium-bodied, with a hint of peat to its flavour, which is smooth and sweet, derived from part-maturation in sherry casks.

One of the newest Scots whisky distilleries (opened in 1974), Auchroisk was built by International Distillers and Vintners and is licensed to Justerini & Brooks. Dorie's Well provides the distillery with its pure, natural water source. The building itself has won several awards, including one from the Angling Foundation for not interfering with the progress of local salmon as they swim upriver. The company has been marketing its single malt since 1987 and it is already a winner of twelve major awards.

SPEYBURN

Speyburn-Glenlivet Distillery, Rothes, Moray

BOTTLING AGE...	10 years	TASTE RATING ...	3–4
STRENGTH.......	40%	MINIATURES	Yes

Tasting Notes

A medium-bodied whisky with a firm yet subtle flavour
and a dry, warming, peaty finish.

Speyburn was built in 1897 on the outskirts of Rothes,
and outwardly has hardly been altered in the past
century. Set among rolling green slopes, it is one of the
most picturesque distilleries in Scotland. It was originally
built for the blenders John Hopkins and later acquired by
United Distillers. Its produce was difficult to find as a
single malt until it was bought from UD in 1992 by the
independent Inver House Distillers, also producers of An
Cnoc, the Pinwinnie blend and Heather Cream liqueur.

SPRINGBANK

Springbank Distillery, Campbeltown, Argyll

BOTTLING AGE . . 12, 15, 21,
25, 30 years

TASTE RATING . 4

STRENGTH 46%

MINIATURES . . Yes

Tasting Notes

A smooth, mellow whisky, light- to medium-bodied with sweet, smoky notes in its flavours.

Springbank was built in 1828 by the Mitchell family, previous owners of an illicit still in the area. The distillery is still owned today by the founders' family, and has never been closed at any time in its history. Along with Glenfiddich, Springbank is unusual in bottling on the premises, and is also the only Scottish distillery to carry out the full malt whisky production process, from floor malting to bottling. Springbank is not coloured with caramel, and is the only malt sold under a distillery label which has not been chill filtered. Longrow single malt is also produced here.

"STRATHISLA"
PURE HIGHLAND MALT
SCOTCH WHISKY
THE OLDEST DISTILLERY IN THE HIGHLANDS
AGED 12 YEARS

STRATHISLA

Strathisla Distillery, Keith, Banffshire

BOTTLING AGE ... 12 years   TASTE RATING ... 4

STRENGTH .... 43%   MINIATURES ..... Yes

Tasting Notes

A big, robust whisky which is full-flavoured and fruity, with a nutty, sherried sweetness.

According to records, production of a 'heather ale' by local clerics had been taking place in this area as early as 1208. The later siting of Milton Distillery (as Strathisla was formerly known) here in the eighteenth century may have been for the same reasons: set in a good barley-producing area, with easy access to a pure local spring which had been a holy well of local Cistercian monks, and said to be guarded by water spirits. The distillery, one of the oldest and most picturesque in the Highlands, passed through several hands until it was bought by Chivas Brothers, a Seagram subsidiary, in 1950.

TALISKER

Talisker Distillery, Carbost, Isle of Skye

| BOTTLING AGE . . . 8, 10 years | TASTE RATING . . . 5 |
| STRENGTH . . . . 45.8% | MINIATURES . . . . . Yes |

Tasting Notes

Talisker is Skye's only malt and has been described as being mid-way between Islay and Highland malts. It is full-bodied with a rich, peaty flavour and elements of malty, fruity sweetness.

Talisker Distillery had an inauspicious start in the 1830s, being denounced by a local minister as a great curse for the area. Despite his disapproval, distilling has continued successfully, with the distillery changing hands several times. A victim of several fires throughout its 160-year history, it was almost completely rebuilt in 1960. The distillery is owned today by United Distillers, and some of its product goes into Johnnie Walker blends. The single malt appears in UD's Classic Malts series, and was even praised by exile Robert Louis Stevenson in his poem, *The Scotsman's Return from Abroad*, as one of 'The King o' drinks'

TAMDHU

Tamdhu Distillery, Knockando, Moray

BOTTLING AGE . . No age given	TASTE RATING . . .	3
STRENGTH 40%, 43%	MINIATURES	Yes

Tasting Notes

A good, light-to-medium Speyside malt, which is slightly peaty but with a delicate sweetness and a long, subtle finish.

Highland Distilleries bought this distillery shortly after it opened in 1897 and have owned it ever since. It was extensively refurbished in the 1970s and is now one of the most modern distilleries on Speyside. Set in the Spey valley, Tamdhu used to favour the hyphenated Glenlivet suffix, but this has been dropped in recent years. As well as its appearance as a single malt, Tamdhu features in The Famous Grouse blend, owned by Highland's subsidiary, Matthew Gloag & Son.

TAMNAVULIN

Tamnavulin Distillery, Tomnavoulin, Banffshire

| BOTTLING AGE... 10 years | TASTE RATING ... 3 |
| STRENGTH...... 40% | MINIATURES ..... Yes |

Tasting Notes

A lightish, mellow Glenlivet-type malt with a sweetish bouquet and taste but an underlying grapey note.

Opened in 1966, this was one of the newest Highland distilleries. A rather functional building, it is set on slopes above the River Livet and used water from a near-by burn. This is another distillery which once carried the hyphenated Glenlivet suffix but has since shed it. Tamnavulin was owned until 1993 by Invergordon Distillers, but Whyte & Mackay acquired the group that year. Since then, production has been mothballed here and at two of the other former Invergordon malt distilleries, Tullibardine and Bruichladdich.

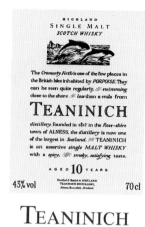

TEANINICH

Teaninich Distillery, Alness, Ross-shire

BOTTLING AGE... 10 years	TASTE RATING ... 3
STRENGTH....... 43%	MINIATURES ..... Yes

Tasting Notes

A difficult-to-find single malt, Teaninich is assertive with a
spicy, smoky and satisfying taste.

Teaninich Distillery dates from the early 1800s and in
1887 it was recorded as the only distillery north of
Inverness to be 'lighted by electricity'. The majority of the
present buildings date from the 1970s and it is now owned
by United Distillers who reopened it in 1990 after it was
mothballed for several years. Most of the production has
traditionally gone into blending, but the single malt has
become easier to find since its official bottling as part of
UD's Distillery (Flora and Fauna) Malts series.

TOBERMORY

Tobermory Distillery, Tobermory, Isle of Mull

BOTTLING AGE... No age given TASTE RATING ... 3

STRENGTH...... 40% MINIATURES..... Yes

Tasting Notes

A nicely balanced, light-to-medium malt with a slightly smoky, flowery aroma and drier, heathery tones in its flavour. A good pre-dinner dram.

Set in a wooded site by the sea, Tobermory Distillery has enjoyed mixed fortunes since it was first established in 1823. It has been closed several times during its existence, most recently in the 1980s when it was mothballed. Having reopened in 1990, the distillery is now back in production. The distillery was previously known as Ledaig, changing its name in the 1970s and a single malt marketed under the old name is also available. Tobermory remains one of the few family-owned independent distilleries.

TOMATIN

Tomatin Distillery, Tomatin, Inverness-shire

BOTTLING AGE . 10, 12, 25 years		TASTE RATING . . 2	
STRENGTH 40%, 43%		MINIATURES . . . . Yes	

Tasting Notes

A lightly peated and delicately flavoured malt, with a smooth, gently spiced finish.

At over 1000 feet above sea level, Tomatin is one of Scotland's highest distilleries. Situated in the Monadhliath Mountains from where it draws its water supply, the distillery was established in 1897 (although it is known that whisky has been made on the site since the sixteenth century). A major programme of expansion in the early 1970s made Tomatin the largest distillery in Scotland and in 1985 it became the first Scotch whisky distillery to have Japanese owners.

TOMINTOUL

Tomintoul Distillery, Ballindalloch, Banffshire

BOTTLING AGE . . . 10 years   TASTE RATING . . . 2–3

STRENGTH . . . . 40%, 43%   MINIATURES . . . . . Yes

Tasting Notes

A light, delicate whisky with a fine balance of sweet and oaky flavours in the Glenlivet style, leading to a nicely smooth finish.

Built in 1964 near to Tomintoul, the second-highest village in Scotland and once a centre for illicit distilling, Tomintoul Distillery is also, at 1100 feet, one of the highest in the country. Its water is drawn from the nearby Ballantruan spring. In spite of its scenic location, surrounded by hills and the Glenlivet forest, it is a modern, functional building which lacks the charm associated with the architecture of many older distilleries. Owned until 1993 by Invergordon Distillers, Tomintoul was one of the group's seven malt distilleries which passed into the hands of Whyte & Mackay that year.

THE TORMORE

The Tormore Distillery, Advie, Moray

BOTTLING AGE... 10 years   TASTE RATING ... 2–3

STRENGTH...... 40%, 43%   MINIATURES..... Yes

Tasting Notes

A medium-bodied whisky, rich, slightly sweet, and nutty in flavour. An after-dinner dram.

Built in 1959, this was Speyside's first new distillery this century. Not a traditional-looking distillery, it is an attractive complex in a pleasant Highland setting, and has the delightfully kitsch touch of a chiming clock which plays the air, *Highland Laddie*, every hour. Tormore's water comes from the Achvochkie Burn, fed by the nearby Loch an Oir (Lake of Gold). An impressive working model of the Tormore Distillery can be seen at the Scotch Whisky Heritage Centre on Edinburgh's Royal Mile. The distillery itself is owned by Allied Distillers, with some of its produce featuring in their Long John blends.

TULLIBARDINE

Tullibardine Distillery, Blackford, Perthshire

BOTTLING AGE . . . 10 years   TASTE RATING . . . 2–3

STRENGTH . . . . 40%   MINIATURES . . . . . Yes

Tasting Notes

A good, all-round single malt, full-bodied and with a smooth, well-rounded flavour with a grapey note.

Tullibardine Distillery was built on the site of a medieval brewery reputed to have produced ale for the coronation of James IV in 1488. It was opened in 1949 and is actually situated at Blackford, a few miles from Tullibardine village. Tullibardine was one of the seven malt distilleries, previously belonging to Invergordon Distillers, which passed into the ownership of Whyte & Mackay in 1993. Since then production has been mothballed.

TYRCONNELL

Cooley Distillery, Dundalk, Co. Louth

STRENGTH . . . . . . 40%   TASTE RATING . . . 2–3

MINIATURES . . . . . Yes

Tasting Notes

The Tyrconnell is smooth, mellow whiskey whose light and sweet taste is complemented by a pleasingly dry finish.

Today produced at the Cooley Distillery, this whiskey was once the prime brand of the Londonderry distillery of A. A. Watt & Co., which was bought out and closed by the Scottish Distillers Company Ltd in 1925. The original Tyrconnell was one of the most popular Irish whiskies in the early twentieth century, and was therefore a fitting candidate for revival recently by its new owners, John Locke & Co. In 1876 the name Tyrconnell was borne by a horse which was owned by the Watt family and entered in the Irish classic race, 'The Queen Victoria Plate'. The horse's victory and its dream odds are still celebrated on its namesake's label today.

COLLINS